MATH IN OUR WORLD

HOW FAR AWAY?

COMPARING

TRIPS

By Jennifer Marrewa

Reading consultant: Susan Nations, M.Ed.,
author/literacy coach/consultant in literacy development
Math consultant: Rhea Stewart, M.A., mathematics content specialist

WEEKLY READER®
PUBLISHING

Please visit our web site at **www.garethstevens.com**
For a free color catalog describing our list of high-quality books,
call 1-800-542-2595 (USA) or 1-800-387-3178 (Canada). Our fax: 1-877-542-2596

Library of Congress Cataloging-in-Publication Data

Marrewa, Jennifer.
    How far away? : comparing trips / Jennifer Marrewa.
        p. cm. — (Math in our world. Level 2)
     ISBN 978-0-8368-9006-8 (lib. bdg.)
     ISBN-10: 0-8368-9006-X (lib. bdg.)
     ISBN 978-0-8368-9015-0 (softcover)
     ISBN-10: 0-8368-9015-9 (softcover)
    1. Distances—Measurement—Juvenile literature. I. Title.
    QC102.M37   2008
    530.8—dc22   2007033382

This edition first published in 2008 by
Weekly Reader® Books
An Imprint of Gareth Stevens Publishing
1 Reader's Digest Road
Pleasantville, NY 10570-7000 USA

Senior Editor: Brian Fitzgerald
Creative Director: Lisa Donovan
Graphic Designer: Alexandria Davis

Photo credits: cover, title page, p. 16 © David Young-Wolff/PhotoEdit; pp. 6, 8, 13 © Royalty-
Free/Corbis; pp. 7, 11 Photos.com; p. 9 © David Muench/Corbis; p. 17 Hiroyuki Matsumoto/
Photographer's Choice/Getty Images; p. 18 © Richard Cummins/Corbis; p. 19 The name and
image of the ELISSA are registered trademarks of Galveston Historical Foundation. All rights
reserved; p. 21© Bill Ingalls/CNP/Corbis; p. 23 © Steve Chenn/Corbis.

Printed in the United States

1 2 3 4 5 6 7 8 9 10 09 08 07

TABLE OF CONTENTS

Words that appear in the glossary are printed in
boldface type the first time they occur in the text.

Chapter 1:

Where Will Maria Go?

Maria's family plans a trip. They look for places to visit. They look for things to do. Maria loves to travel. She meets new people. She learns new things.

Maria lives in Los Angeles, California. She wants to visit a zoo. She wants to go to a museum. Her family likes those places, too. They look at a map to plan their trip.

Maria's mom **compares** the **distances** to both places. The zoo is in San Diego. San Diego is 116 miles from their home. The museum is in Santa Barbara. Santa Barbara is 105 miles from their home.

Distance from Maria's home to the zoo	116 miles
Distance from Maria's home to the museum	105 miles

The distance from Maria's home to the zoo is **greater than** the distance from her home to the museum. 116 is greater than 105. Maria's family thinks about other places they might visit near the zoo. They also think about other places near the museum.

7

If her family goes to the zoo, they will visit San Diego. They will visit Old Town. They also will go to San Diego Bay. Maria wants to look for shells on the bay's beach.

If her family visits the museum, they will go to Santa Barbara. They will visit a painted cave at a state park. The Chumash Indians made drawings there. Some of the art is hundreds of years old. They will spend a day at the beach, too. Maria loves to swim.

On the Way to San Diego!

Maria's family must pick one city to visit.
Maria's family plans to go to San Diego. Their
first stop is the zoo. The San Diego Zoo is one
of the largest zoos in the world. More than four
million people visit the zoo each year.

The zoo is in a park. There are many kinds of animals. Maria likes the apes the best. She watches one hide its face. Her brother waves to the ape. The ape does not wave back. It is ready for a nap.

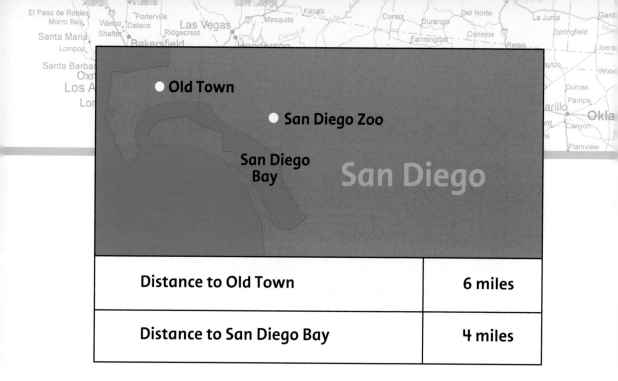

Distance to Old Town	6 miles
Distance to San Diego Bay	4 miles

Maria's family decides where to go next. They could see Old Town. There is a park there. They could go to the bay. It is sometimes called the Big Bay. Old Town is 6 miles from them. The bay is 4 miles away. Maria's family decides to visit the bay.

San Diego

Maria buys a postcard. She sends it to her cousin Juan. She tells him about the places they visited. She tells him that she liked the bay the best. "See you soon!" she writes.

Chapter 3:
Where Will Juan Go?

Juan's family plans a trip. They look for places to visit. They look for things to do. Like his cousin Maria, Juan loves to travel.

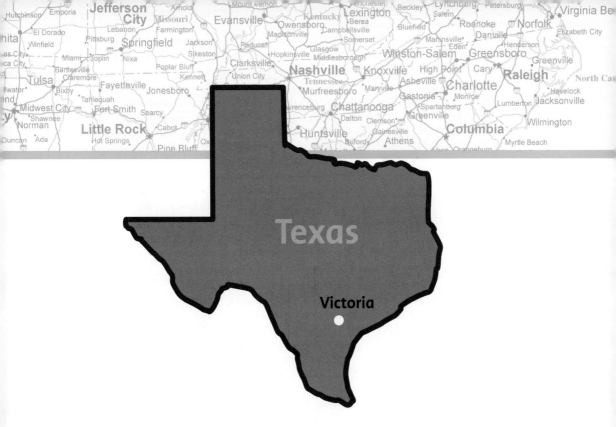

Juan lives in Victoria, Texas. He wants to see the space center. Juan wants to explore space when he grows up. He also wants to visit an aquarium. Juan's family likes those places, too.

Juan's dad compares the distances to both places.
The Johnson Space Center is in Houston. Houston
is 129 miles from their home. The aquarium is in
Galveston. Galveston is 169 miles from home.

Distance from Juan's home to the space center	129 miles
Distance from Juan's home to the aquarium	169 miles

From Juan's home, the distance to the space center is **less than** the distance to the aquarium. 129 is less than 169. The space center is closer to Juan's home.

If Juan's family goes to the space center, they will visit Houston. They will go to the Museum of Natural Science, too. They will also spend time at a lake. Juan wants to ride in a boat there.

If his family visits the aquarium, they will go to Galveston. They will go to the Texas Seaport Museum. They will also spend time at the beach.

Chapter 4:
Off to Houston!

Juan's family plans to go to Houston. They stop at the Johnson Space Center first. Juan is excited to see the center. The center trains space explorers.

Juan's family sees a space shuttle. Juan learns about a space day camp. He likes the Mission Control Center the best.

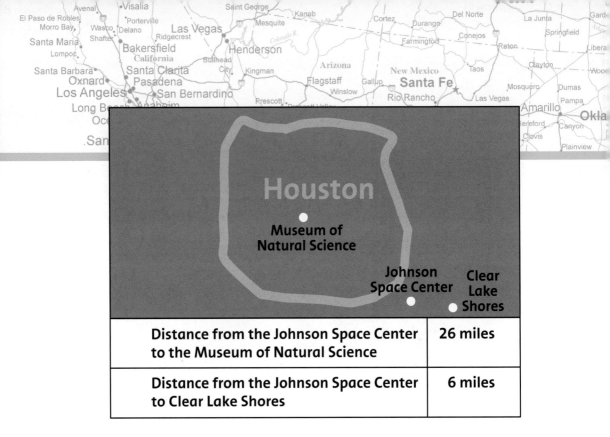

Distance from the Johnson Space Center to the Museum of Natural Science	26 miles
Distance from the Johnson Space Center to Clear Lake Shores	6 miles

Juan's family decides where to go next. They could visit the museum or go to the lake. The museum is 26 miles from the space center. The lake is 6 miles away. The lake is closer, but it is raining. Juan's family decides to visit the museum.

Juan buys a postcard. He sends it to his cousin Maria. He tells her about the places they visited. He tells her about the space center. "Wish you were here," he writes.

Glossary

compare: to find ways in which two or more things are alike and different

distance: the length of space between two points

greater than: a larger amount than something else. 116 is greater than 105.

less than: a smaller amount than something else. 129 is less than 169.

About the Author

Jennifer Marrewa is a former elementary school teacher who writes children's books, poetry, nonfiction, and supplemental learning materials. She lives in California with her husband and two young children.